Key West Houses

Key West Houses

Leslie Linsley
Photographs by Jon Aron

RIZZOLI
NEW YORK

First published in the United States of America in 1992 by
Rizzoli International Publications, Inc.
300 Park Avenue South
New York, NY 10010

Copyright © 1992 Rizzoli International Publications
Text copyright © 1992 Leslie Linsley
Photographs copyright © 1992 Jon Aron
Reprint 2000, 2001, 2003

Library of Congress Cataloging-in-Publication Data

Linsley, Leslie
    Key West houses / Leslie Linsley; photographs, Jon Aron.
        p.   cm.
    Includes bibliographical references and index.
    ISBN 0-8478-1494-7
    1. Architecture, Domestic—Florida—Key West.   2. Architecture,
Tropical—Florida—Key West.   3. Vernacular architecture—Florida—
Key West.   4. Key West (Fla.)—Buildings, structures, etc.
I. Aron, Jon.   II. Title.
NA7238.K48L56   1992
728'.37'0975941—dc20   91-28698
                                                        CIP

PAGE 1
Pineapple cut-outs, 613
Simonton Street.

FRONTISPIECE
Weather-worn façade,
Bahama Town.

OPPOSITE
Gable detail, 531 Caroline
Street.

FRONT COVER
The Southernmost House, at
1400 Duval Street, built in
1900.

BACK COVER
Left: Roof detail, The Albury
House, 730 Southard Street.
Right: Conch house, 907
Angela Street.

DESIGNED BY PAMELA FOGG
DESIGN ASSISTANT: BETTY LEW
MAP DRAWN BY T.R. LUNDQUIST
Manufactured in China

Contents

Acknowledgments

We extend our thanks to the following people who have generously given us their time and help and have graciously allowed us to photograph their homes: Larry Bauerle, Richard K. Champney, Walton Cox, Dominic Fabis, Carole and Gerald Fauth, Richard Gardiner, Tripp Hoffman, Lynn and David Kaufelt, Pat and Philip Timyan, Holly Tyson, and Alan Van Wieren.

We also thank those who were especially helpful in other ways: Shirley Block, Alec Harding, and Sandy O'Brien. Special thanks to Jim Blum of The Real Estate Company of Key West, Inc., Barbara Haas of Classic Travel, and to American Airlines for assistance with travel arrangements.

Most of all we thank our good friends Carol and Karl Lindquist, who enabled us to become intimate with Key West through their eyes, for always extending their friendship and hospitality. The experience has made Key West a part of us forever.

Leslie Linsley and Jon Aron

RIGHT
A common method of expanding a small house was to add one or more ells at the back of an exisiting structure. Some houses on the island have as many as four of these "sawtooth" additions. This house is located on Olivia Street. Photograph by Carol Lindquist.

OPPOSITE
Elaborately detailed covered poorches and sun deck adorn the building at 1327 Duval Street.

Map of Key West

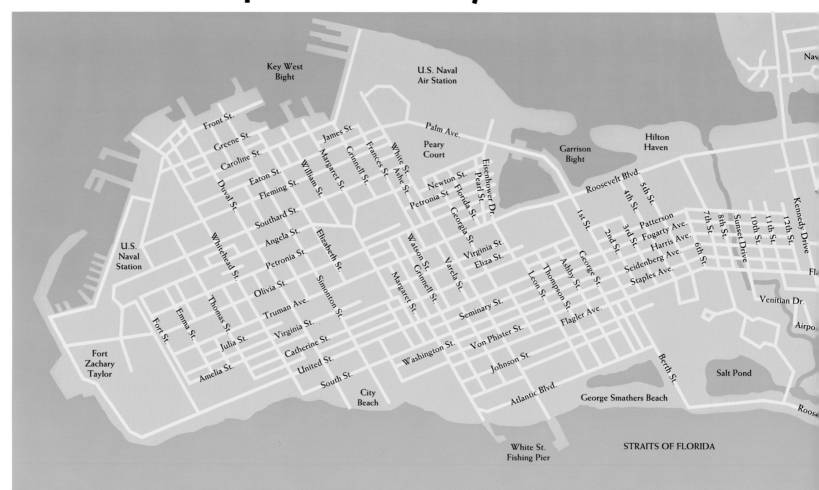

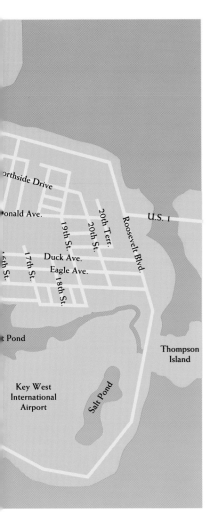

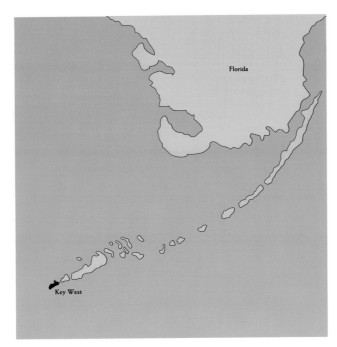

Northside Drive

onald Ave.

20th Terr.

20th St.

19th St.

18th St.

17th St.

16th St.

Duck Ave.

Eagle Ave.

Roosevelt Blvd.

U.S. 1

Thompson Island

Pond

Salt Pond

Key West International Airport

Florida

Key West

Introduction

"**F**orty-two degrees in Dallas, six degrees in New York City, snowing from Maine to Washington. The only warm place in the entire country on this January day is Key West, Florida, with a high of eighty-two. Even Miami is experiencing an unusual cold spell of fifty-six degrees." A morning-radio weather report during the winter simply confirms what most inhabitants of the southernmost tip of the continental United States already know: Key West is a tropical paradise. But the consistently ideal climate is only a part of what attracts so many people to this island, which is rich with cultural history, architectural interest, and natural beauty.

Located 150 miles south of Miami and ninety miles north of Cuba, Key West is only four miles long and one mile wide and, for the most part, is surrounded by a coral reef. It is inhabited by over 35,000 permanent residents and plays host to over two million visitors from around the world each year.

Key West boasts a colorful history. In 1815 King Ferdinand VII of Spain gave the island to infantryman Juan Pablo Salas, as a reward for unspecified military services. In 1821, while living in Havana, Cuba, Salas sold the property for two thousand dollars to an American financier, John Simonton, whom he met in a bar. Being a savvy businessman, Simonton immediately sold off portions of the island to fellow businessmen John Fleming, John Whitehead, and Pardon Greene, who ultimately became prominent citizens of Key West. Streets in the portion of the island known as Old Town are named for all these gentlemen.

Key West was an ideal location for an international port. Though surrounded by coral reefs, ships could travel easily through four channels leading to its natural har-

ABOVE
A buoy marks the southernmost point in the continental United States.

BELOW
The Wrecker's Museum is located in the oldest house in Key West. Its builder was a ship's carpenter from the Bahamas who originally constructed the house at the corner of White-head and Caroline Streets before it was moved to its present site at 322 Duval. It was once the home of a sea captain, who eccentrically added dormers of varying sizes.

bor. Simonton was aware of the island's strategic position. Through his influential friends in Washington, he was able to establish Key West as an American port of entry, a sure means of building an economy. Simultaneously, an outbreak of piracy in the area caused the loss of many lives and cargo and threatened the growing economy on the island. Once again, Simonton used his government contacts to get help. In 1822, when Florida was ceded to the United States, the Federal government took possession of Key West. Four years later, a naval base was established on the island in order to rid the surrounding waters of pirates. For the next 150 years a major portion of the island's land area was devoted to United States Navy operations.

In 1828 the settlement at Key West was incorporated as a city. The first houses were built in a cluster on the northwestern tip of the island. By 1831, there were eighty-one residential and commercial buildings in Key West. The population hovered at 360.

During the nineteenth century, sea traffic making its way from Havana through the treacherous, reef-filled waters surrounding Key West created a "wrecker's paradise." Many of the island's early settlers, who had been New England seafarers, saw the financial possibilities in salvaging cargo from ships wrecked on the coral reefs. There were plenty of shipwrecks each year to support a good portion of the island's population in the salvage business. Indeed, many of the grandest Key West houses were built from the wood salvaged from the wrecked ships, and were furnished with items from the fine cargo found on board. To organize the wrecking industry, the United States government established a court on the island to determine the value of the salvaged cargo. Washington also passed a law requiring all ships wrecked in American waters be brought to the nearest American port. As a result, the wrecking business in the British colony of the Bahamas dropped considerably. Many ambitious Bahamian wreckers moved to Key West to pursue their livelihood, becoming American citizens. Wrecking became big business on the island, reaching a high point in 1855. As the nineteenth century progressed, however, several lighthouses were built to mark the reefs, greatly reducing the number of shipwrecks off Key West. The wrecking business slowly died out.

At the same time, sponging and turtling were also thriving businesses. Until the 1960s, when the sea turtle was declared an endangered species and turtling was outlawed in the United States, Key West provided most of America's turtle-based products. The soft underbelly of the turtle was used to make soups, burgers, steaks, and chowders. The first processed turtle soup was canned in Key West in 1895. The development of the sponging industry attracted Bahamian wreckers and fishermen who settled in Key West. By 1892, 8,000 of Key West's 25,000 residents were of Bahamian origin.

Just three years after the end of the American Civil War, Spanish dominance over Cuba ignited a revolutionary struggle that started a ten-year war. Many Cubans fled

their country for the nearest friendly port—Key West. They arrived bringing an industry with them, the manufacturing of handmade cigars. The first cigar factory on the island had been established in 1831 on Front Street. By the late nineteenth century there were 166 cigar factories in Key West employing thousands of workers, many of Cuban origin. Over 100 million cigars a year were produced. The growth of the cigar-making business provided employment and increased revenues in the city, so that by 1880 Key West was not only the wealthiest city per capita in the United States but the largest city in Florida. Also, since it could not be reached by land, Key West was visited by more American ships than all other southern United States ports combined.

All this activity and affluence brought about an overwhelming demand for housing. Over the years, those who came to Key West from the Bahamas, Cuba, Europe, and the eastern seaboard of the United States introduced a wide variety of building styles. As a result of this mix of architectural styles and the common use of wood as a building material, the buildings in Key West are distinct from those in other Florida cities.

Wood was brought to Key West and became the primary material employed in the construction of its houses. Some of the lumber used for home building was salvaged from the hulls of wrecked ships; some lumber, from Pensacola in the north, was found as cargo on wrecks. More affluent builders spent their earnings from other industries importing mahogany from Honduras, buying cypress from the Upper Keys, and purchasing pine from other Gulf Coast ports. Very few of the original houses were built with plaster, which would crack if the building shifted in a high wind or hurricane. The interior walls of houses also were constructed of wood. Dade County pine strips were often placed horizontally to form paneled walls, in a way similar to the means of finishing the interior of a boat. The island's Historic District includes 3,000 wooden structures that have been listed on the National Register of Historic Places.

Any simple wooden residence in Key West is known as a Conch house and reveals much about the island's past. The earliest settlers from the Bahamas were particularly fond of eating conch (pronounced konk), a giant sea snail eaten raw in salads or deep fried in batter to create the delicacy known locally as a conch fritter. Over the years conch has come to describe anything native to Key West, including its citizens and their charming houses with wide front porches and louvered windows.

Most of the early houses were built without the aid of a professional architect and, more often than not, designed as construction progressed. The early builders

drew on their memories of other buildings and construction methods with which they were familiar. Those who had been ships' carpenters incorporated such practical conveniences as roof hatches for ventilation. Sea captains from New England often built sturdy, well-proportioned structures with double-hung sash windows. Widow's walks, so popular in coastal towns in New England, are seen atop the grander Key West houses along the waterfront.

The taste for Victorian architecture that swept the country during the latter part of the nineteenth century was incorporated into the design of many houses in Key West. Corner brackets, balustrades, porch columns, and fretwork fences, among other ornamental details, were applied to the rather spare conch-style houses.

The enormous growth of the cigar-making industry in Key West required affordable housing for thousands of factory workers. Small, unpretentious, single-story houses were erected close together on lots near the factories. Just as the larger homes on the island were built in the Victorian and Bahamian styles, these simple frame houses borrowed elements from those styles as well. Similar building techniques and local materials were employed and, while humble in appearance, these more modest homes are not overshadowed by the grand wrecker's houses in Old Town. The small houses found dotting streets and lanes throughout Key West contribute greatly to the charm and intimate atmosphere of the city as a whole.

Along with the growth of residential construction, the commercial district of Key West also experienced a construction boom, slowed only in 1886 when an uncontrollable fire swept through the entire wooden commercial district. Wharfs, warehouses, factories, stores, and City Hall were destroyed. However, business was hardly affected: sponging, cigar making, salvage and wrecking, fishing, and retailing operations continued to thrive and the commercial district was quickly rebuilt.

In 1891 the Naval Commandant's Quarters, known as "The Little White House," was built on the local naval base. Built as officers' quarters, it was later used by visiting presidents. Only President Harry S. Truman actually stayed overnight in the building and, having fallen in love with Key West, returned ten times. It was said that he enjoyed visiting the island because he could walk through the streets undisturbed. Truman's presence brought Key West to the attention of the public and assisted in establishing the island as a tourist destination. The Little White House is now a museum.

In 1904, retired oil baron Henry Flagler, who is well known for his development of the resort city of Palm Beach, announced plans to build a railroad from Miami to Cuba. Key West would be linked by land to the rest of Florida for the first time. By 1912 Flagler's Overseas Railroad, which required the building of hundreds of oversea bridges in order to connect all the Florida Keys, reached its last American stop, Key West. Its construction cost over fifty million dollars and 700 lives. Flagler died a year after its completion. The railroad connection to Cuba was never to be realized. With the overland connection, the population of Key West grew to 23,000.

Building Styles in Key West

CLASSIC REVIVAL: THREE BAY, CENTER HALL

Built either with a roof line parallel to the street or, as is most common in Key West, with its gable end facing the street, this type of one-and-a-half-story structure is usually constructed with a covered front porch supported by four square columns. Inside, the rooms are arranged off a central hall. These houses often were built with a small rear wing. As is the case with many Key West houses, the structure is supported by a foundation of sunken piers, leaving space for air circulation beneath its floors. Roof scuttles, oversize window shutters, and decorative balustrades are typical embellishments.

CLASSIC REVIVAL: THREE BAY, SIDE HALL

The most common wooden house type in Key West is the three bay, temple-form house with its gable end situated on the street side of the lot. Approximately one third of the examples of this house type on Key West are one-and-half-story structures, as shown. If there is a stairway to a second level, it is located in the side hall. In many existing examples on the island, owners have altered interiors to make use of limited space. The version shown in this drawing has standard, double-hung, wooden sash windows without shutters, and an attached, covered front porch.

CLASSIC REVIVAL: EYEBROW

The front façade on this type of two-story house continues up behind the roof overhang supported by six columns. The second-story windows are partially covered by the roof. This regional building type is well suited to the climate of a tropical island: the roof shades the second story from the strong rays of the year-round sun.

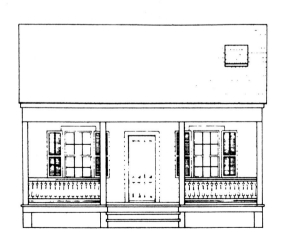

CLASSIC REVIVAL: THREE BAY, TWO STORY

This type of side-hall-plan house offers details that show more classic inspiration than structures characterized by their spare use of decorative motifs. Its cornice is well defined, windows and doors are pedimented, and porch columns have simple decorative capitals. A steep roof is a common sight in Key West. Rain water was collected from the run off, which may explain why, with the exception of roof scuttles, there are few roof structures seen on the island's houses. Only a few of the grander houses offer dormers, cupolas, and widow's walks.

CLASSIC REVIVAL: FIVE BAY, CENTER HALL

The larger wooden houses on Key West were built with the same vocabulary of decorative details as the smaller houses. Nineteenth-century builders had a penchant for formal balance and symmetry. This type of two-story house, with its roof line parallel to the street, offers a good example of the more formal style of Key West residences. The five bays are of equal width. Doors and windows on the first floor are aligned with those on the second floor. Foundation piers, porch columns, and roof scuttles also are arranged symmetrically.

SHOTGUN

This kind of house is a rectangular, one-story, wood-frame structure, a single room wide. The roof ridge is always perpendicular to the street. Often no more than twelve by thirty feet, several of these houses, built initially to house the growing worker population of Key West, could be placed on a small lot. Most explanations of the derivation of the term "shotgun" used to describe this type of house involve the alignment of front, back, and interior doors to create a continuous passage through the house, one in which a bullet could pass without hitting an interior wall. This building style was common in the southern United States during the late nineteenth century.

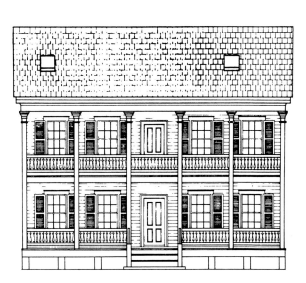

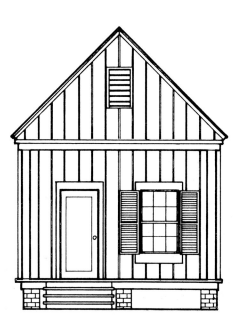

The 1920s saw the exhaustion of the sponging industry in Key West. An influx of fun-loving tourists discovered the island. Soon the small, quick boats that had been used for sponging and wrecking were carrying bootleg whisky to Key West from Havana. The roaring twenties were a high time on the island.

The Great Depression of the 1930s brought the wild times of the 1920s to an end. Key West's businesses slumped. The cigar-making business on the island began to dwindle. Beset with labor problems, the cigar makers moved their factories north to Tampa, attracted by that city's better transportation and distribution facilities and cheaper labor. Tourists stopped coming and the railroad approached bankruptcy. In 1935 a major hurricane destroyed so much of the railroad that for three years the island was cut off from the mainland once again. Federal funds were used to convert the railroad bridges to a two-lane highway. The automobile and truck connection did much to revive Key West's economy, making the island easily accessible to post-war American tourists.

In the late 1940s, the jumbo Gulf shrimp, known locally as "pink gold," was discovered quite by accident. Until then, shrimpers had set out trawling nets but had only come up with unimpressive catches. One day a shrimp boat was stranded at sea. During the night, the crew of the boat put out their nets to pass the time. In the morning their nets were full of large shrimp. It turned out that the shrimp did not like the light that penetrated the clear waters and only came to the surface at night. This discovery established an important industry that has survived to this day. In the post-war years, with tourism increasing, sportfishing became one of Key West's greatest attractions. The Gulf waters are filled with barracuda, sailfish, marlin, yellow and blackfin tuna, dolphin, bonefish, grouper, snapper, and mackerel.

Writers and artists have always been lured by the "end of the line." This tip of America, rich with natural beauty, is one of the most romantic areas of the country. Key West's most famous residents were Ernest Hemingway and Tennessee Williams. They attracted an enclave of creative people to the island and their presence still is felt throughout the city today: bookstores promote their works as if they were current releases; their homes are tourist attractions; information put out by the city of Key West includes anecdotes and reported stories about them; the post office branch sells posters of the Hemingway stamp; a local bar advertises the fact that Hemingway drank there; and the community theater regularly performs Williams's plays. Key West is still a writer's town: eight Pulitzer prize-winning writers reside on the island. It is rumored that there are more writers than bars in town.

Over the years Key West has suffered from many natural and human disasters—hurricanes, fires, its loss of the cigar business—which have created dramatic economic ups and downs. These fluctuations and the island's remote location have been its best protection against modern building developments that might have destroyed its architectural character. Throughout the Old Town one sees, in dramatic juxtapo-

MARGARET-TRUMAN
DROP-OFF LAUNDERETTE

The San Carlos Institute, at 516 Duval Street, was the political and social center for the island's Cuban community in the nineteenth century, and remains an important site for Cuban visitors. It is now open as a museum, and events such as the annual Key West Literary Seminar are held there. It is a fine example of Spanish-influenced architecture in Key West.

The Casa Marina Hotel was built by the Flagler chain and opened on New Year's Eve, 1920. The Mediterranean-style resort hotel stands on expansive grounds with a 500-foot beachfront. The Marriott Corporation has restored the hotel, which had fallen on hard times over the decades, to its former grandeur.

BELOW
Some residents of Key West live in houseboats of varied designs. This example is one of many located along Roosevelt Boulevard, known as "Houseboat Row."

sition, elaborate Queen Anne-style homes built at the turn of the century, little Louisiana Creole cottages, ornate Victorians, and the houses categorized as "Key West Tropical" in style, to which the unmistakable combination of decorative motifs is applied. Every street, boulevard, and lane is rich with architectural variations and contradictions.

After 1974, when the navy closed its base in Key West, the city focused its attention on the tourist trade. In the process of attracting more tourists, the island's residents and businesspeople concentrated on sprucing up for visitors, which included a movement toward the restoration of public and private buildings. And, while gay people have long appreciated Key West's unique and open atmosphere, in the mid-1970s the city experienced an influx of businesses owned by gay people. Boutiques, guest houses, hotels, bars, restaurants, and organized gay cruises have contributed to the island's economy. At the end of the 1970s, almost seventy percent of all restoration and renovation was accomplished by gay people. Their presence has contributed to the relaxed and tolerant attitude that is enjoyed by all who visit or live there.

The recent wave of gentrification on the island comes with an enlightened awareness of Key West's richest treasures. Registration as a National Historic District in 1982 has helped with the preservation of Key West's Old Town. Guidelines for preservation are made available by the Historic Architectural Review Commission, active as an architectural review board for the historic district of the City of Key West and the Historic Florida Keys Preservation Board. Old Island Days House and Garden Tours each year help to promote the appreciation of Key West architecture.

Key West is exciting, sophisticated, eccentric, and eclectic. Even at its most grown-up and serious, when night falls over the island tiny Christmas tree lights add sparkle everywhere. The decorative touch of whimsy lights the way up garden paths, blinks on and off around welcoming doorways, adds a festive mood to fences, twinkles around swimming pools, and beckons from swaying palm fronds. No manufactured perfume can compete with the heavy scent of jasmine, gardenias and frangipani that fills the air. The slightest breeze unleashes the aroma of orange blossoms, and fuchsia-colored bougainvillea winds its way over trellises to brighten the façades of the houses.

Key West is always changing, but its residents are doing their best to keep the pace slow. Most locals and visitors agree that it is like no other place on earth, and they like it that way. Where else is the celebration of sunset cause for the entire population to congregate at the old Mallory dock at the end of each day?

RIGHT
Pepe's, a waterfront café housed in a vernacular storefront, is popular with Key West locals and visitors.

BELOW
The Kress Building, at the corner of Duval and Fleming Streets in downtown Key West, opened in 1913 as the site of the local five-and-dime. In 1978 it became Fast Buck Freddie's, the island's closest answer to a department store.

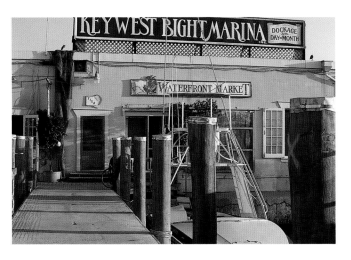

ABOVE
The Waterfront Market, at 201 William Street, was once the Singleton Shrimp Packing Company. It is now a hub of activity, with fresh fish offered daily along with an array of cheeses, fruits, and vegetables.

ABOVE RIGHT
Sloppy Joe's, the island's oldest and most famous bar, was the favorite hangout of Ernest Hemingway and other artists and writers. In 1962, a year after Hemingway's death, part of the original manuscript of *To Have and Have Not* and the great writer's notes on *A Farewell To Arms* were found in the saloon's back room.

BELOW RIGHT
These turtle *kraals,* or holding pens, are all that remain from one of Key West's bygone industries.

Architectural Details

The variety of building styles in Key West is a result of the blending of cultures, ideas, and construction techniques. The architectural details that were popular during the nineteenth century in other areas of the United States were applied in one form or another to houses in Key West—sometimes a number of them appear on one house! Whether the stylistic influence is Classic Revival, West Indian, Folk, Victorian, or Queen Anne, the Key West version is generally smaller, simpler, and less ornate than comparable houses built in other regions.

LEFT
The houses of Key West offer a rich array of distinctively designed architectural details.

OPPOSITE
The use of window shutters came to the island from the Bahamas. Hinged on the side or top, they can be closed for protection during hurricanes and tropical storms. Louvers can be adjusted to admit cooling breezes while controlling the effects of the sun's rays.

LEFT
The metal roof became a common sight on the island during the early nineteenth century when sheet iron became available. Coated with tin to inhibit rust, the metal was fabricated in sheets or shingles. The preferred roof coverings in Key West today are embossed shingles or sheets of galvanized metal coated with aluminum paint to prevent rust and contribute to thermal efficiency.

RIGHT
Gingerbread decorations can be seen throughout Key West applied to all styles of residences. These elaborately carved details appear on a house at 313 William Street.

Porches, verandas, and balconies abound in Key West. First- and second-story wraparound verandas are a common sight, as at 313 William Street. Many buildings do not have a first-floor porch, but instead have one which spans the façade across the upper story. These covered outdoor spaces are an important part of tropical living.

LEFT
Rooftop cupolas, turrets, and towers are typical elements of the large Queen Anne-style houses on the island. The tower atop The Artist Guest House, at 534 Eaton Street, is a fine example.

ABOVE
Balustrade details at 1327 Duval Street.

ABOVE RIGHT
The entrances to Key West houses are characteristically simple, with details selected from elements in the classical vocabulary. Porch supports of turned spindles with modest capitals or square columns with simple moldings are most commonly seen. Shutters flank the entrance door at 823 Eaton Street.

RIGHT
Most Classic Revival-style houses are temple-form, with the gable end oriented toward the street. Frequently the gables are punctuated with gingerbread trimming, decorative windows, or fanciful verge boards.

OPPOSITE
Exterior stairways are features found on some of the larger houses, often leading to a second-floor gallery or roof terrace. A typical example can be seen at 912 Fleming Street.

Romantic Creations

The Queen Anne and Victorian styles arrived in Key West during the late nineteenth century and were immediately embraced by builders. At the turn of the century, the city was prospering, and several wealthy citizens built expansive houses in these romantic styles. Although the styles originated in England, they seemed to fit perfectly then, as they do now, in tropical Key West. The gingerbread trim gives even the most formal house a playful appearance.

But beneath the fairy-tale exterior, the house was solidly built. The use of the modern balloon frame, in which walls were built of closely spaced studs running from the floor joists to the roof plate, allowed walls to be raised in one piece. A house could be erected by two men in less time than it took twenty to build a house with the traditional timber construction method.

Each example of this style of house is unique. Extravagant details—octagonal towers, turrets, varied roof levels, dramatic projecting bays, balconies with balustrades, generously wide, wrap-around porches, and filigree work reminiscent of wedding cake decoration—give each house its own eccentric character. And eccentricity has always been a personality trait associated with the people who live in Key West.

ABOVE
Built in 1890, this Classic Revival building, at 1001 Eaton Street, was the home of the Cuban consul to the United States in 1906. It was remodeled in 1912, with verandas, a rear bay, and a gingerbread-trimmed circular gallery added. The unabashed mixing of styles is typical on Key West houses.

OPPOSITE
In 1900 George A.T. Roberts, who had moved to Key West from the Bahamas, built the house at 313 William Street, considered to be the island's most outstanding example of the Queen Anne style. A double veranda snakes around the house, which has been restored by its present owners, Tripp Hoffman and Alan Van Wieren.

RIGHT
The architectural detailing of the poolside gazebo on the Roberts property is reflective of that on the main house.

OPPOSITE
The rear façade of the Roberts house is rather plain in comparison to its "full dress" street façade.

ABOVE
Victorian-period scenes are etched in the glass panels around the elaborately carved door of The Artist Guest House.

OPPOSITE
"The Southernmost House," at 1400 Duval Street, was built in 1900 by one of Key West's prominent citizens, Judge J. Vining Harris. His wife, Florida, was the youngest daughter of William Curry. This colorful brick house is typically Queen Anne, with an irregular interior plan and an array of dormers, ells, towers, and other construction details that animate the façade. In the 1940s the house became the Casa Cayo Hueso Supper Club until it was sold to Hilario Ramos. He restored it to use as a private residence in 1952.

ABOVE
The Queen Anne-style residence at 534 Eaton Street was built in 1898 for Thomas Otto, Jr. Having undergone extensive restoration, it is now The Artist Guest House. Its exterior offers a blend of stylistic features.

OPPOSITE
The Octagon House, at 712 Eaton Street, was built by Richard Peacon in 1899. Only a few thousand houses of this shape were built in the United States, mostly in New York, Massachusetts, and the Midwest. The house was once owned by the well-known interior designer Angelo Donghia, who purchased it in 1974 for forty-five thousand dollars. He spent over one hundred thousand dollars renovating and redecorating the house and in 1980 sold it to the fashion designer Calvin Klein for almost a million dollars, the highest price ever paid for a house in Key West at the time.

ABOVE
The master bedroom in the Octagon House opens onto the second-floor veranda.

RIGHT
The wide, wraparound porch leads to a pedimented entranceway at the side of the house. The front door is framed by a transom window and louvered shutters.

The rear of the Octagon House is a complete surprise, with its pared-down Greek Revival look. Glass-paneled doors across the back of the house fold open on the lush gardens and pool area.

ABOVE
On the house's second level, off the master
bedroom, is a pleasant private veranda.

OPPOSITE
An upstairs bathroom in the Octagon House was remodeled in the 1970s, but its original Dade County pine paneling was left intact. A porthole window in the shower wall provides a view of the surrounding treetops.

ABOVE
The octagonal shape of the house is reflected in the sitting room, where the Dade County pine paneling has been pickled to a light tone. Tall windows are framed with Federal-style moldings. Shutters are used to adjust the level of light and to provide privacy from the busy street outside. The ceiling fan is a typical interior element in houses on Key West. Even in the most luxurious homes air conditioners are rarely used.

LEFT
A graceful stairway leads to the second and third floors. The combination of stain and paint on the balusters emphasizes their decorative carving.

The house's gingerbread details cast shadows that create an ever-changing lacelike pattern on the façade.

The Gingerbread House, a pink confection at 615 Elizabeth Street, is considered the best example of Victorian gingerbread on the island. It is more "folk" than Victorian since the basic structure, a simple two-story building consisting of five bays and a center hall, would not evoke the Victorian style without its gingerbread mill-work. The house was built in 1885 by a leading Key West merchant, Benjamin P. Baker, as a wedding gift for his daughter. He owned the local bake shop around the corner and his profession may have influenced the design of the house, which some refer to as a "wedding cake."

ABOVE
The Victorian-style house at 524 Francis Street was built circa 1907 by carpenter-architect William Kennedy, who also designed the Curry Mansion. The house sits at the head of Stump Lane in a neighborhood noted for its typically nineteenth-century flavor. Under the seven-gabled tin roof, the wealth of period details includes dentils, moldings, cornices, and porches on all sides. In 1989 the house was renovated by its current owners, real-estate agent and author Lynn Mitsuko Kaufelt and her husband, novelist David Kaufelt.

RIGHT
The side porch offers a private outdoor living space, an essential part of many Key West residences.

ABOVE
The large front porch invites one to sit and catch the cool Gulf breezes. Tropical plantings, including banana trees, yellow and pink hibiscus, orange and red ginger, deep red bougainvillea, and white birds of paradise, surround the house.

RIGHT
The underside of the porch roof is painted cool aqua. Louvered Bahamian shutters, painted in a dark tone, cover the large windows of the house.

LEFT
When renovating this house, the Kaufelts were able to retain as much of its original interior detailing as possible, while opening up the plan for modern living requirements.

ABOVE
The moldings and plaster walls—rare in Key West—were painstakingly restored to their original beauty.

RIGHT
Touches of color punctuate the interior, in which the architectural details have been emphasized. A handmade newel post with spherical cap is the focal point of the stair hall.

Gingerbread

The introduction of the scroll saw and turning lathe in the nineteenth century inspired a diversity of decorative architectural millwork. The resulting gingerbread trim can be seen on the houses on any street in Old Town, Key West, and lends a Victorian air to even the most humble cottage.

Gingerbread detailing is used to decorate porches, gables, balustrades, and columns. A decorated façade may be reminiscent of a lacy valentine or a wedding cake, though few houses in Key West are heavily embellished. Most often the gingerbread trim is just enough to make a plain house a little fancier. While this type of millwork was mass produced, many carpenters created their own designs. The façades of Key West houses offer a wide variety of one-of-a-kind decorative detail.

LEFT
Decorative balustrades, fences, and other gingerbread details can be found on houses throughout Old Town.

OPPOSITE
Decorated verge boards identify this small house as Gothic Revival in style.

ABOVE
While most of the houses in Key West are
painted white, the unpainted façades have
a charm of their own.

RIGHT
A weather-beaten gable decoration.

ABOVE
The pineapple has always been a symbol of welcome and hospitality. This cut out baluster frames an outdoor stairway at 613 Simonton Street.

LEFT
Lacy corner brackets adorn simple porch posts on many Key West residences.

RIGHT
Spindlework friezes appear between porch columns on even the most modest houses.

OPPOSITE
Jigsaw cutouts of simple forms dress up a white wooden house in Old Town.

Small Houses

Most of the small houses of Key West were built during the last quarter of the nineteenth century. They often were erected quickly to meet the prevailing need to house the growing population of cigar factory workers. These simple houses, known as shotguns, face onto the street with façades pierced only by a single door and window. Typically, these one-and-a-half story houses were made of wood, and featured little or no decorative detail. The original dwellings were comprised of three narrow rooms in a row leading back from the front of the building. The front, rear, and interior doors were aligned, which is supposedly why this type of house is called a shotgun. One could fire a shot from the open front door right through the house and out through the back door.

There are few of these houses left intact. Over the decades, owners have often added a side hall or another front window, to create a more comfortable flow in terms of plan, light, or ventilation. Where space allows, rooms have been added or expanded. The best examples of shotgun houses can be seen in a concentrated area on Olivia, Watson, Varela, and Packer Streets.

LEFT
While most Key West houses are painted white, some have been painted in pastel tones, such as the elegantly renovated shotgun house at 623 Frances Street.

OPPOSITE
A typical Conch house at 612 Elizabeth Street in Old Town.

LEFT
The row of shotgun houses on Truman Street were built to house cigar workers during the 1870s and 1880s. These basic wooden buildings offered compact rooms and were placed side by side, with their gable ends facing the street. Though many of these houses have been purchased and remodeled by newcomers, native Conch families still own almost half of the original shotgun houses in Key West.

ABOVE

Most Key West cottages were built with the gable end facing the street, in order to maximize the number of house lots on a block. It is unusual to find houses placed broadside on a generous lot. These houses, at 905 and 907 Angela Street, are virtually unchanged from when they were built.

LEFT

In shotgun houses the front and back doors are aligned at either end of a long hallway. The interior walls of this house, at 726 Fleming Street, are covered with sandblasted Dade County pine.

RIGHT

It is rare to find an unpainted, untouched Conch house, such as at 907 Angela Street. Porch swings are a common sight in Key West.

ABOVE
The late-nineteenth-century house at 608 Angela Street was owned by writer-actor Phillip Burton. The house is weather-stripped, creating one of the most arresting "naked houses" of Key West.

RIGHT
This quaint shotgun house, at 314 William Street, is right at home on a street that boasts grand Victorian and Bahamian houses. It is one of many single-bay frame structures scattered throughout Old Town.

OPPOSITE
The house at 619 Ashe Street is structurally similar to the Burton residence. However, it has a different kind of presence because of its freshly painted exterior.

LEFT
The Tennessee Williams house, at 1431 Duncan Street, is a modest, one-story clapboard structure almost completely hidden by surrounding foliage. The famous playwright came to Key West in 1941 because of its remote location. Williams initially lived in a boarding house, later moving to the La Concha Hotel, on the corner of Duval and Fleming Streets, where he worked on *Summer and Smoke.* In 1949 he decided to make Key West his home and bought this old Bahamian house, where he lived until his death in 1983. *The Rose Tattoo,* for which he won a Pulitzer Prize, was written in this house, furnished with old wicker Williams bought in Cuba.

RIGHT
Because of his admiration for the writer Jane Bowles, Williams built a gazebo in her memory on the property. The letters of the writer's nickname, Tom (his given name was Thomas Lanier), were carved into the gazebo's gingerbread fretwork.

OPPOSITE
418 William Street has the classic proportions of a small frame house with its roof ridge parallel to the street.

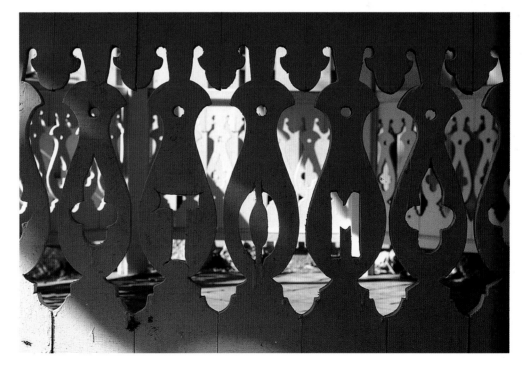

59

ABOVE AND LEFT
The small Conch house at 1318 Angela Street
has been restored and given an imaginative
paint job.

OPPOSITE
A typical small house at 511 Margaret Street.

SYZYGY

625

OPPOSITE
Owner Holly Tyson completely renovated the shotgun house at 625 Francis Street. The renovation included the addition of a second-floor room. One-and-a-half-story buildings in Key West typically have a window for ventilation in the gable end facing the street.

LEFT
In this small house, walls were removed to create a more spacious living area. The ceiling is covered in rattan and rafters have been left exposed. Bamboo furnishings, unusual artifacts, and blossoming orchids create a tropical ambience. French doors open to the deck and pool, surrounded by lush foliage.

ABOVE
A long hallway is always found in early shotgun houses. The stairway was added during the house's renovation and leads to a small room on the second floor.

ABOVE
This painted stairway is a feature of the renovated pair of side-hall houses on Petronia Street.

ABOVE RIGHT
1406 and 1408 Petronia Street are two of three sister houses built circa 1900. They exemplify the type of house the average Key West family lived in at the time. The owners, Wally Cox and Richard Gardner, joined the two houses, building a patio and shared pool between them. The grounds are planted with bright pink hibiscus, palm trees, and other tropical foliage.

RIGHT
French doors in the living room open on to the pool area in the back of 1406 Petronia Street. Sunburst transoms were custom made.

For years Love Lane was an enclave of the descendants of Alexander Roberts, who owned the whole square block. Small streets such as this one are common in Key West. Many writers have lived in the little Conch house at 712 Love Lane. William Wright bought and remodeled the house and added a small garden. Russell Baker and David Halberstam each rented the house for a season. The current owners, cookbook authors Carol and Karl Lindquist, turned the front yard into an enchanting environment with a brick-and-stone patio and overhead trellis laden with cascading bougainvillea.

ABOVE
At the end of the center hall is an orchid porch. Pickled wood flooring is light and practical, in keeping with the overall environment of the house. The owners collect paintings by Jack Baron, a local artist.

LEFT
A mini-jungle of tropical plants and trees creates a natural wall around the property, providing complete privacy in Old Town, where the houses are built close to one another.

ABOVE
In the bedroom, pine walls have been softened with a whitewash, allowing the natural pink of the wood to show through. Louvered doors lead to the pool deck.

Cutouts

Keyhole saws provided the means by which Key West craftspeople and homeowners creatively personalized their houses. Simple shapes were cut into wooden window shutters and fence pickets. Recognizable shapes adorning the exterior of a house often symbolized the resident's hobbies or means of making a living. It was considered in poor taste to copy a neighbor's cutout designs, so on a stroll down a Key West street one encounters a range of charming and often amusing cutout motifs.

LEFT
Carved apples decorate the posts at the building that houses the Southernmost Signs Service at 913 Eaton Street.

OPPOSITE
Three lucky stars adorn the gable of a house at 580 William Street.

ABOVE AND RIGHT
A fence in Old Town features cutouts of
pineapples, a traditional symbol of welcome.

OPPOSITE
A row of gingerbread men appears on the
façade at 1020 Southard Street. The design
may have been chosen by a previous owner
in the bakery business.

ABOVE
The bottles in the decorative balustrade at 1117 Duval Street refer to the building's past use as a speakeasy.

LEFT
Sailboat, sun, and seagull cutouts create a graceful design on either side of the porch posts at 618 Ashe Street.

ABOVE
An intricate, rhythmic pattern of fish can be
seen on the porch posts at 926 Southard Street.

RIGHT
A musician or music teacher must have
commissioned the violin cutouts that adorn
every column on the porch at 514 Francis Street.

Bahamian Influences

When a United States law specified that salvaged cargo from shipwrecks in Amercan water be brought to the nearest domestic port, the wrecking industry in Key West was given a boost. Many wreckers from the Bahamas relocated to the island. They brought their own architectural style with them. The traditional Bahamian house was well suited to a tropical climate and such devices as window louvers and roof hatches for ventilation became part of the Key West architectural vocabulary. The houses were built on limestone pier foundations so that cool air could circulate underneath the floorboards. Downspouts and gutters were used to collect rain water in cisterns. Wide porches and second-story balconies were built to provide additional living space during especially hot weather.

Wooden shingles had been used to roof houses on the island until the Bahamians introduced metal roofs, which reflected the sun's rays and heat. Picket fences, while part the New England landscape, are thought to be of Bahamian origin in Key West, as are double-hung windows and low roof overhangs. Perhaps the most significant import from the Bahamas was the ceiling fan, the kind associated with classic films like *Key Largo*. One can hear the lazy hum of the fans stirring the air ever so slightly in houses, public buildings, and even garden gazebos all over Key West.

ABOVE
Few Key West houses have prominent roof features. The Albury House, at 730 Southard Street, offers a well-preserved New England-style widow's walk.

OPPOSITE
In 1847 Captain Richard Roberts, known as "Tuggy," came to Key West from Green Turtle Cay in the Bahamas, bringing his disassembled house with him. Reassembled, it stands on its original site at 408 William Street.

The RICHARD ROBERTS HOUSE
MOVED TO ✺ KEY WEST
From Green Turtle Cay, Bahamas
· in 1847 ·

This unadorned building at 610 White Street serves as an office for an architect specializing in Old Town building renovations.

LEFT
The Roberts House, at 408 William Street, is Bahamian in style and offers unique "beaded" siding. The shaded verandas extend the long dimension of the house on both its levels. Built by master craftsmen, it has outdoor stairways, roof scuttles, wide plank floors, and mahogany-trimmed window sashes. The house has survived three hurricanes. Roberts married three times and produced enough offspring to keep the house in one family until 1964.

OPPOSITE
Built in the second half of the nineteenth century, the William Albury house, at 730 Southard Street, incorporates many typical conch features: wraparound porches, attic window vents, a stone pier foundation, and an array of eclectic decorative details.

LEFT
The formalism of Classic Revival architecture is evident in the house at 1009 Windsor Lane, though this example offers a four-bay façade rather than the more common three- or five-bay façade. The first record of this house dates to 1912, when it was located at 1008 William Street. The current owners, Pat and Philip Timyan, restored the house with the help of architect Bert Bender, best known for his restoration of the Key West Lighthouse.

OPPOSITE
The Samuel Filer house, at 724 Eaton Street, was designed by William Kerr, one of Key West's finest architects during the nineteenth century.

This house, located at 620 Southard Street, was originally built by John Lowe, Jr. in 1855. Lowe's father made a fortune as a wrecker and owned a fleet of sponge and lumber ships. This early Bahamian-influenced villa was built with heart of pine and Honduras mahogany joined with wooden pegs. The widow's walk offers views of both the Atlantic Ocean and Gulf of Mexico.

OPPOSITE
Colours Guest House, at 410 Fleming Street, was built in 1874 by a Cuban tobacco entrepreneur, Francisco Marrero, who made his fortune in less than fifteen years after bribing his way out of a Havana jail.

RIGHT
The Sawyer/Navarro house, built circa 1870, is a conch landmark offering thirteen grand rooms, high ceilings, and ornately sculpted moldings. It was moved from Duval Street to its present site, 426 Elizabeth Street.

ABOVE
The most common window type in Key West is the double-hung wooden sash, with six lights in each sash. These examples are at 615½ Whitehead Street.

RIGHT
The conch-style building at 615½ Whitehead Street has a Classic Revival-style structure. It features a two-story porch with turned columns and balusters. The original wood clapboard siding, windows, and nineteenth-century balloon frame construction were preserved in the award-winning restoration of the building, which now serves as law offices.

OPPOSITE
The Red Doors is an old waterfront landmark at the corner of William and Caroline Streets. Built in 1868 by the Pinder and Curry families, the building was initially a cigar factory. When the island's cigar-making business moved to Tampa, the building became a ship's chandlery then a grocery store, a shrimper's bar, changing its name often until it became the Red Doors tavern. The "Doors" earned an unsavory reputation as a frequent site of fights, stabbings, even murders, and was dubbed the "Bucket of Blood." Today it houses an art gallery, antique shop and the Caroline Street Bookstore.

Built in 1873, the two-story house at 701 Fleming Street is one of two "sister" houses built by L.E. Pierce for his daughters. This stately home, opposite the Monroe County Library, was once owned by composer-lyricist Jerry Herman. Great care and excellent craftsmanship have gone into the renovation of this wonderful structure with its wraparound porches, complex series of ells, and unusual roof line.

1107 Fleming Street offers an excellent example of the formalism of Classic Revival houses. It has a five-bay façade with a centered entry door, creating the desired bilateral symmetry. The central-hall plan creates a balanced interior as well, with two rooms off either side of the entrance hall.

A watch tower stands between the main house and guest cottage at 1617 White Street.

The large house at 1617 White Street is an example of a new building incorporating the traditional Key West architectural vocabulary. The wooden structure, owned by Gerald and Carole Fauth, brings New England and Bahamian influences together: large, shuttered windows, expansive porches, and a watch tower, from which one has a spectacular view of the Atlantic Ocean.

The absence of walls between rooms creates an easy flow from one living area to the next. The high ceilings, overhead fans, screenless windows, and internal louvers between rooms were designed for optimum air circulation. The wicker furniture was collected one piece at a time in flea markets, antiques and secondhand shops from all over the United States.

ABOVE
The louvered window shutters and the porch spanning the façade of the house were adopted from Bahamian models.

Raised Eyebrows

An unusual type of revival-style residence in Key West is charmingly referred to as an Eyebrow house. While there are thirty examples of such houses in Key West, they do not exist anywhere else in Florida. The roof eaves extend well below the top of the façade, shading the upper story of the house. The low roof line also serves to catch cool breezes and deliver them to the rooms inside. The "eye" windows on the second story are the same size as those on the first floor, but are partially hidden behind the overhanging roof "brow." While only a view of the front porch is provided from these windows, the rooms receive plenty of indirect sunlight during the day.

LEFT
In this small Eyebrow house at 525 Francis Street, the large pedimented windows may seem out of scale, but they are necessary for air circulation. The overhanging roof eave shades the upstairs windows.

OPPOSITE
The restored house at 823 Eaton Street offers shuttered windows, door pediment, columns, and balustrade — all typical Eyebrow details.

Curved corner brackets in a sunburst pattern
form arches between the porch columns on this
Eyebrow house.

Every device for catching a breeze is used in this
house at 1121 Southard Street. There are two
windows at the gable end, shutters close against
the direct heat of the sun, and a roof hatch
affords ventilation.

OPPOSITE
The large Eyebrow house at 512 William Street is painted in pastel tones, as are many Bahamian-style residences on Key West.

ABOVE
This pretty, rather formal-looking Eyebrow house at 643 William Street, with pedimented door and windows, was built in 1880 by Edward Roberts, a ship's carpenter. The tall columns are topped with scrollwork that softens the design.

Selected Bibliography

Cox, Christopher. *A Key West Companion.* New York: St. Martin's Press, 1983.

Kaufelt, Lynn Mitsuko. *Key West Writers and Their Houses.* Englewood, FL: Pineapple Press, 1986.

Langley, Joan and Wright. Key West Images of the Past. Key West, FL: Key West Images of the Past, Inc., 1982.

McGarry, Richard. *Key West Sketchbook, A Slice of the Island Life.* Key West, FL: Maupin House, 1990.

Nichols, Stephen. *A Chronological History of Key West.* Key West, FL: Key West Images of the Past, Inc., 1989.

Wells, Sharon and Lawson Little. *Portraits: Wooden Houses of Key West.* Key West, FL: Historic Key West Preservation Boards, 1979, 1991.

Williams, Joy. *The Florida Keys, A History and Guide.* New York: Random House, 1991 (updated yearly).

Resources

Conch Tour Train
601 Duval Street
Key West, FL 33041
(305) 294-5161
Sightseeing tours

Key West Chamber of Commerce
Old Mallory Square
Key West, FL 33041
(305) 294-2587

Key West Island Book Store
513 Fleming Street
Key West, FL 33040
(305) 294-2904
A section of this store is devoted to
Key West writers and local subjects.

Key West Welcome Center
3840 North Roosevelt Boulevard
Key West, FL 33041
(800) 284-4482
Referral service for hotel, motel,
and restaurant reservations.

Lower Keys Chamber of Commerce
Overseas Highway, Mile Marker 31
Big Pine Key, FL 33043
(800) 872-3722

Monroe County Public Library
700 Fleming Street
Key West, FL 33040
(305) 294-8488
A section of the library is devoted to
Key West history and local authors.

Old Town Trolley Tours
1910 North Roosevelt Boulevard
Key West, FL 33041
(305) 296-6688
Sightseeing tours

Pelican Path: A Guide to Old Key West
The Old Island Restoration
Foundation, Inc.
P.O. Box 689
Key West, FL 33041
(305) 294-9501
Visitors can pick up this guide and map
at the Hospitality House in Mallory
Square. Fifty-one points of interest with-
in walking distance are highlighted.

Solares Hill Walking and Biking
Guide To Old Key West
Solares Hill Publications
1217 White Street
Key West, FL 33041

(305) 294-3602
This give-away paper, written by
Sharon Wells, is a must while in Key
West and is available throughout
the island.

Tourist Development Council
of Key West
416 Fleming Street
Key West, FL 33041
(305) 296-2228

Walden Books
2122 Roosevelt Boulevard
Key West, FL 33040
(305) 294-5419
A section of this store features
regional and local books.

Writer's Walk
Key West Literary Seminar, Inc.
(305) 745-3640
A one-hour, one-mile guided tour
of Key West author's houses and
gathering places.

Index